My Home Country

CANADA

IS MY HOME

For a free color catalog describing Gareth Stevens' list of high-quality books, call 1-800-341-3569 (USA) or 1-800-461-9120 (Canada).

For their help in the preparation of *Canada Is My Home,* the writer and editor gratefully thank the Dennis family, Murray and Sandy Wright and their family, and John Saunders.

Picture credits: Covers, pp. 22-23, 32, courtesy of the Dennis family; pp. 8-9, The Metro Toronto Convention & Visitors Association; pp. 18-19, © 1991, Gareth Stevens, Inc.; p. 33 (middle, bottom), Tourism New Brunswick, Canada; pp. 33 (upper), Industry, Science and Technology Canada Photo; p. 48 (flag illustration), © Flag Research Center.

Library of Congress Cataloging-in-Publication Data

Wright, David K.
      Canada is my home / adapted from David Wright's Children of the world--Canada by David Wright : photographs by David Wright.
          p. cm. -- (My home country)
      Includes bibliographical references and index.
      Summary: A look at the life of an eleven-year-old Canadian girl and her family as they move from Toronto to Halifax. Includes a section with information on Canada.
      ISBN 0-8368-0846-0
      1. Canada--Juvenile literature. 2. Canada--Geography--Juvenile literature. [1. Family life--Canada. 2. Canada.] I. Wright, David K. Canada. II. Title. III. Series.
      F1008.2.W76   1992
      971--dc20   92-17726

Edited, designed, and produced by

Gareth Stevens Publishing
1555 North RiverCenter Drive, Suite 201
Milwaukee, Wisconsin 53212, USA

Text, photographs, and format © 1992 by Gareth Stevens, Inc. First published in the United States and Canada in 1992 by Gareth Stevens, Inc. This U.S. edition is abridged from *Children of the World: Canada,* © 1991 by Gareth Stevens, Inc., with text and photographs by David K. Wright.

Series editor: Beth Karpfinger
Cover design: Kristi Ludwig
Designer: Beth Karpfinger
Map design: Sheri Gibbs

Printed in the United States of America

1 2 3 4 5 6 7 8 9 97 96 95 94 93 92

My Home Country

CANADA
IS MY HOME

Adapted from
Children of the World: Canada
by David K. Wright
Photographs by David K. Wright

Gareth Stevens Publishing
MILWAUKEE

After living near a lake for most of her life, Rachel's backyard now ends on the ocean. Her family has moved from a town close to Toronto, in the middle of Canada, to the far eastern coast of this enormous country. Despite the move, Rachel's enthusiasm for rhythmic gymnastics remains. While she misses her friends and especially her gymnastics coach back near Toronto, Rachel adapts well to her new home, school, and friends, particularly her new Labrador puppy.

To enhance this book's value in libraries and classrooms, clear and simple reference sections include up-to-date information about Canada's geography, demographics, languages, currency, education, culture, industry, and natural resources. *Canada Is My Home* also features a large and colorful map, bibliography, a glossary, simple index, and research topics and activity projects designed especially for young readers.

The living conditions and experiences of children in Canada vary according to economic, environmental, and ethnic circumstances. The reference sections help bring to life for young readers the diversity and richness of the culture and heritage of Canada.

My Home Country includes the following titles:

Canada	*Nicaragua*
Costa Rica	*Peru*
Cuba	*Poland*
El Salvador	*Vietnam*
Guatemala	*Zambia*
Ireland	

CONTENTS

LIVING IN CANADA:
Rachel, a Girl on the Move

This is Rachel Dennis. She is 11 years old and in sixth grade. Rachel lives near Halifax, Nova Scotia, where her backyard faces the Atlantic Ocean! Rachel has a father, Paul, and a mother, Rhonda. She has one brother, Greg. He is eight and in the fourth grade.

Many Canadians move. Rachel's story begins far from her home, in Toronto. . . .

Rachel Dennis enjoys a sunny summer day. ▸

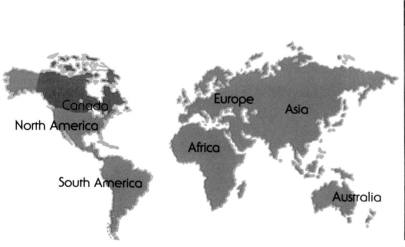

Toronto is one of Canada's largest cities.

A Big Decision

Six months ago, no one in the Dennis family could have imagined moving. They lived in a big, new brick home near Toronto. Toronto is one of Canada's biggest cities. It is the capital of the province of Ontario.

This is Rachel's family. Her dad's name is Paul. Her mother's name is Rhonda. Greg is her eight-year-old brother.

The kitchen is a gathering place for the Dennis family.

One day, Rachel's grandfather called from Halifax. He asked if Rachel's father would like a new job. Rachel's dad could be his own boss in a family-owned business. But the Dennis family would have to move east.

Did they want to move? They all loved their large, modern home. Rachel's mother ran a busy household. She was involved in Rachel and Greg's activities.

Rachel's father had worked his way up in his company. Would he quit his Toronto job?

The Dennises and a friend like big plates of spaghetti.

**Above: Rachel trains in a gym near her home.
Left: Greg waits for a pitch. The Toronto Blue Jays are his favorite team.**

Greg was on a soft-ball team. Both children had many friends, but Rachel did not see them often. She spent hours practicing rhythmic gymnastics.

What is Rhythmic Gymastics?

When Rachel was a small child, she loved to play on the jungle gym. Every-one said she looked like a gymnast.

Rachel began ballet classes at age five. She danced for a year, then joined a gymnastics class. She learned to do somersaults, back flips, and other hard moves. But at age eight, it stopped being fun.

Rachel spins a ribbon and tries to stand very straight.

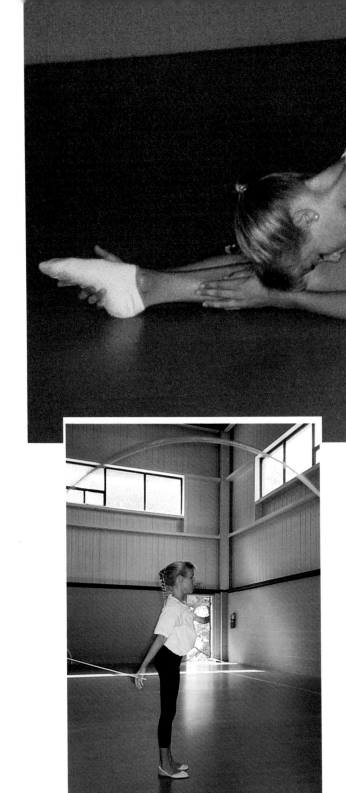

Above: Can you do a split? This is easy for Rachel.
Right: She loves to skip rope.

"I was scared," she says. She saw rhythmic gymnastics on television and signed up for training. The classes let her play with balls, hoops, ribbons, and ropes.

Above: Toni is Rachel's coach. She explains how to perform with a hoop.

Right: Toni shows Rachel how to move.

Rhythmic gymnastics is only for girls. The world's best rhythmic gymnasts are from Eastern Europe. One of them is Rachel's coach, Toni.

Toni is from Bulgaria. She moved to Canada to teach gymnastics and to earn money.

Rachel spent a year with Toni as her coach. "She really did like me, but she expected a lot," Rachel says. Rachel knew that Toni would help her perform.

Rachel trains 12 hours a week during the school year and 15 hours a week in the summer. She is small and light for her age, but she still has to watch her diet!

Rachel's left foot is at six o'clock and her right foot at noon!

The Diet of Champions

Rachel hardly ever eats junk food. Instead, she enjoys spaghetti, pizza, chicken, hamburgers, hot dogs, trout, or tuna. Her mother encourages her to eat bread and vegetables. They give her energy without putting extra weight on her.

Some Canadians speak English, others speak French, and some speak both. Every can, jar, box, and wrapper is printed in both English and French.

Rachel eats a quick breakfast.

AROMA Nº 1

JACOBS Café

Beau Jardin
Raspberry Preserves
NET WT. 13 OZ. (366 G.)

new creamier
SKIPPY
CREAMY
peanut butter

COW BRAND.
baking soda
SODIUM BICARBONATE U.S.P

bicarbonate de soude
BICARBONATE DE SODIUM U.S.P   500g

Fleur de Lait
NEUFCHATEL CHEESE
with
Herb & Spice

NOUVEAU
HYPOSODIQUE

NET 300 g (10.6 oz)

LOW SALT

Petit Beurre
FRENCH
BUTTER BISCUITS

NET WT.
28 OZ.

THE LITTLE SCHOOL
LE PETIT ECOLIER
Butter Biscuits Topped with
Pure Milk Chocolate
& Hazelnuts

A Big School

School is four blocks
away. The name of
Rachel's school is
Regency Acres Public
School. Rachel's
room is in one of the
mobile classrooms.

Regency Acres Public School is a large, modern building.

Rachel likes school.
Her favorite subjects
are language arts and
music. Rachel says she wants to be a
teacher. She also wants to be in the
Olympic Games, but her mother says she
doesn't train enough.

School starts in September and ends in
June. The school day begins at 9:00 a.m.
and ends at 3:30 p.m.

Rachel and Greg walk to school with neighbors. ▸

Rachel and her classmates learn language arts, mathematics, history, music, and art. She also takes social studies, science, and French. Every public school student in Canada learns French.

Canada, the largest country in area on earth, has over 27 million people. That means Canada has only 6 people per square mile (2.3 per sq km). China has 288 people per square mile (111 per sq km)!

My fifth grade class i

My best frog catch ever!

Rowing with Julie-Anne near my new home.

My new best friend, Julie-Anne.

What a meet, what a team!

Rachel's photo album shows her with friends.

Rachel runs to get her kite in the air.

Today, the children are flying kites they have made. Getting a kite to stay up isn't easy when there isn't much wind.

The maple leaf is Canada's symbol.

Rachel and her friends love the jungle gym.

The children eat lunch in a hurry. Rachel says she likes "anything but peanut butter-and-honey sandwiches." A sandwich, an apple, two cookies, and milk fill her up.

While most boys play baseball, Rachel and her friends play tag on the jungle gym.

Rachel and Greg love to visit amusement parks.

Summer Fun

Rachel's parents want their children to be happy during the move. Both children love amusement parks, so the Dennis family goes to one for the day. Rachel rides every ride she can find.

But Rachel's dad and mom are worried. They are afraid their house won't sell.

Rachel's father may have to go to Halifax by himself for a while. But just as it seems that their home will never sell, they find a buyer.

Left: Rachel and her family and friends wait in line for a ride.

Below: The Dennis family has finally sold their house!

Last Days in Aurora

The family has many things to do before moving day. Toni works Rachel very hard. She wants Rachel to remember everything she has learned at the gym. Toni tells Rachel that she has found an apartment. Soon, her husband will join her. They will teach gymnastics together.

Rachel flops on the floor to catch her breath during hard training.

Rachel eats a quick lunch. Then, just for fun, she jumps on the trampoline.

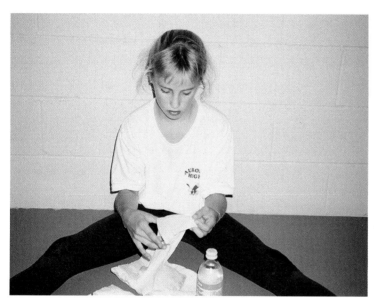

Above: Rachel and Toni work with long ribbons.

Left: Lunch at the gym is a sandwich and a soft drink.

Right: Rachel jumps on a trampoline after lunch.

Rachel loves Robbie's little horses.

After practice, Rachel goes home with
Robbie, who takes lessons in another part
of the gym. The two became friends because
they both like gymnastics.

Robbie lives on a farm and has lots of
animals. Rachel and Robbie ride his all-
terrain vehicle, hop on his trampoline, and
then take a swim in the pool.

Robbie gives Rachel a ride.

Rachel just loves trampolines!

Robbie and Rachel will miss each other when Rachel moves.

The day is warm, so the children swim in Robbie's pool.

A Move, a New Home

Rachel will miss Toni, too. She wants to return to Toronto to train. Rachel's mother knows that she hasn't seen Halifax. She knows Rachel will have fun there, too.

The Dennis family watches movers pack their belongings. Then, they hop in the car for 22 hours of driving.

Movers empty Rachel's house in Toronto.

Above: The St. Lawrence River flows toward Rachel's new home in Halifax.

Right: Rachel can read the French highway signs.

They follow the big Trans-Canada Highway. It follows the St. Lawrence River, which flows toward the Atlantic Ocean.

This is the area where Rachel now lives.

This pretty scene shows the Dennis home and boathouse. It's very different from Toronto!

Rachel's new home is on a cove about 15 miles (24 km) west of Halifax. The home has a boat, a boathouse, and a very beautiful view.

Rachel's dad takes the children out in the boat. Greg and Rachel can hardly wait! It is old and needs some repairs, but it is fun to drive. The only problem is, it won't fit in the boathouse!

Greg and Rachel must put on life jackets before their father takes them for a boat ride.

Boutiliers Point School

After a quick breakfast, Rachel and Greg comb their hair, brush their teeth, and get their homework together. Then, they swing on a rope with Patrick, their new friend, until the bus comes.

Rachel and Greg swing as they wait for the school bus.

They run for the bus. The ride lasts 15 minutes.

Rachel and Greg attend Boutiliers Point School. Rachel has made friends fast, but Greg is shy. "Some of these kids play tackle basketball," he says.

Rachel's classes include the following: social studies, science, writing, reading, math, health, physical education, art, French, and band.

Rachel's sixth-grade class.

Social studies is fun. Several students who enjoy camping out wonder if they could ever live like the Micmac Indians.

Later, the students read silently. Rachel reads *Charlotte's Web,* her favorite.

Rachel's teacher, Mrs. McIsaac, reads to the children.

The students read silently every day.

Rachel and some friends sit on a guardrail during recess.

At recess, Rachel and three friends run up the hill above the school. They nibble snacks and sit on a guardrail. The day is warm and sunny. Rachel can almost see her new house on the ocean. She is beginning to feel at home in Nova Scotia.

MORE FACTS ABOUT: Canada

Official Name: Canada

Capital: Ottawa (OTT-uh-WAH)

History

The first humans in Canada came from Asia. They walked into the country across a strip of land that is now under water. For thousands of years, these people wandered across Canada. They met European explorers on the Atlantic Coast. The explorers came from Britain and France. Soon, British farmers and French fur trappers settled in much of eastern Canada. The natives joined the French against the British and were defeated in a huge battle in Quebec. The victorious British kept moving west, building houses and farming. Far to the north, gold was discovered in the Klondike. As the country was settled, Britain gave Canadians more control. Canada's armed forces helped Britain and the Allies win victories in Europe in World War I and World War II. Canada has ten provinces and two territories and is independent of Britain. With the breakup of the Soviet Union, Canada is now the largest country on earth.

Land and Climate

Half of Canada is covered with forests. The earth is fertile in Ontario and in the west, where crops of corn, wheat, and other grains and vegetables grow. Winters are long and cold, and summers are short and warm. Winter days can be as cold as -70° F (-57° C). The country has many fresh-water lakes, streams, and rivers.

People and Language

Canada is a bilingual country. That means everyone speaks either English or French or both. Almost half of Canada is of English descent. One person in four is of French descent. French is spoken more than English only in Quebec. Canada's minority population includes Inuits and other Native Canadians.

Education

There are two school systems in Canada — the Public School System and the Roman Catholic Separate School Board. Some schools teach in English and some teach in French. In Quebec, all English-speaking children must learn French. Public schools offer kindergarten plus 12 grades of education — except in Ontario. There, children take an extra year of high school.

Religion

Half of all Canadians are Roman Catholic. Most of the rest are Protestant. One Canadian in 10 has no religious preference. About one in 20 is a member of a non-Christian religion.

Sports and Recreation

What is the national sport of Canada? If you guessed ice hockey — you're wrong! Hockey is the most popular sport, but the official national sport is lacrosse. It was first played by Native Canadians. They used sticks with cupped nets on one end to catch and throw a ball. There are two teams. Each tries to score goals in the other's net. Besides hockey, big-league sports include baseball and football.

The queen of Great Britain is on some Canadian bills and on all current coins, including the new $1 coin, which replaced the $1 bill.

More Books About Canada

Canada. Bender (Silver Burdett)
Canada. Law (Chelsea House)
Canada. Sirimarco (Rourke)

Glossary of New Words

bilingual: being able to speak two languages.

Klondike: an area in the Yukon Territory in northwestern Canada. The Klondike is just east of Alaska.

lacrosse: a sport played by two teams with sticks, goals, and a ball.

province: a territory that is part of a country. In the U.S., such territories are called states.

Quebec: a province in Canada where French is the official language. English is often understood but not widely spoken.

Things To Do

1. Could your parent drive in Quebec? That is where the street signs are all in French. Which street sign would be the first one you should learn? Why?

2. Which oceans border Canada?

3. From what you know of both countries, how do you think Canadians are like Americans?

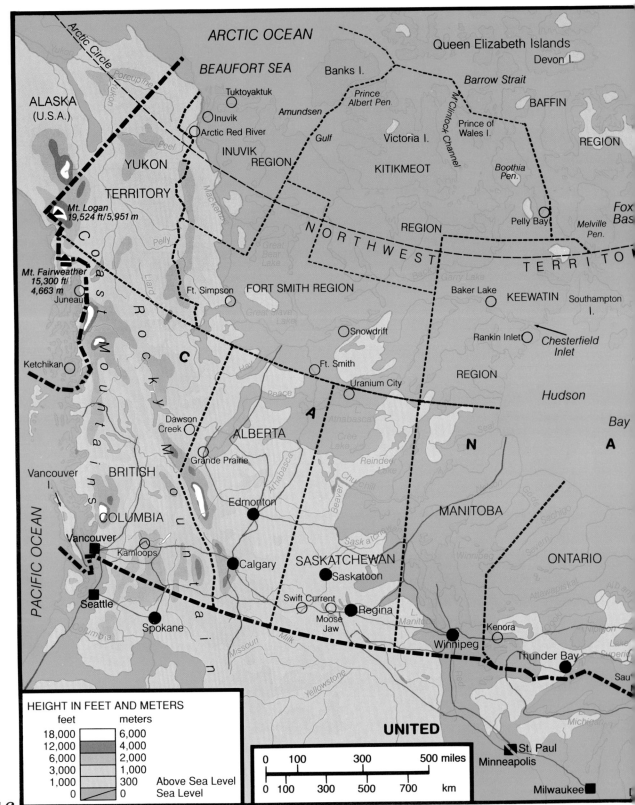

ARCTIC OCEAN

BEAUFORT SEA

Banks I.

Queen Elizabeth Islands

Devon I.

Barrow Strait

ALASKA
(U.S.A.)

Tuktoyaktuk ○

○ Inuvik
○ Arctic Red River

Amundsen

*Prince
Albert Pen.*

BAFFIN

REGION

Gulf

Victoria I.

*Prince of
Wales I.*

YUKON

INUVIK

REGION

KITIKMEOT

TERRITORY

*Boothia
Pen.*

*Mt. Logan
19,524 ft/5,951 m*

REGION

*Melville
Pen.*

Pelly Bay ○

Fox
Bas

*Mt. Fairweather
15,300 ft/
4,663 m*
Juneau

N O R T H W E S T

T E R R I T O

Ft. Simpson ○

FORT SMITH REGION

Baker Lake ○

KEEWATIN

Southampton
I.

Ketchikan ○

○ Snowdrift

Rankin Inlet ○

*Chesterfield
Inlet*

Ft. Smith ○

REGION

Hudson

Uranium City ○

Dawson
Creek ○

ALBERTA

Bay

A

A

Grande Prairie ○

N

BRITISH

Edmonton ●

MANITOBA

Vancouver
I.

COLUMBIA

Vancouver ■

Kamloops ○

MOOSE

Calgary ●

SASKATCHEWAN

ONTARIO

Saskatoon ●

Seattle ■

Swift Current ◐

Regina ●

Spokane ●

Moose
Jaw

Kenora ○

Winnipeg ●

Thunder Bay ●

Sau

PACIFIC OCEAN

HEIGHT IN FEET AND METERS

feet	meters
18,000	6,000
12,000	4,000
6,000	2,000
3,000	1,000
1,000	300
0	0

Above Sea Level

Sea Level

UNITED

0	100	300	500 miles

St. Paul
Minneapolis

0	100	300	500	700	km

Milwaukee ■

46

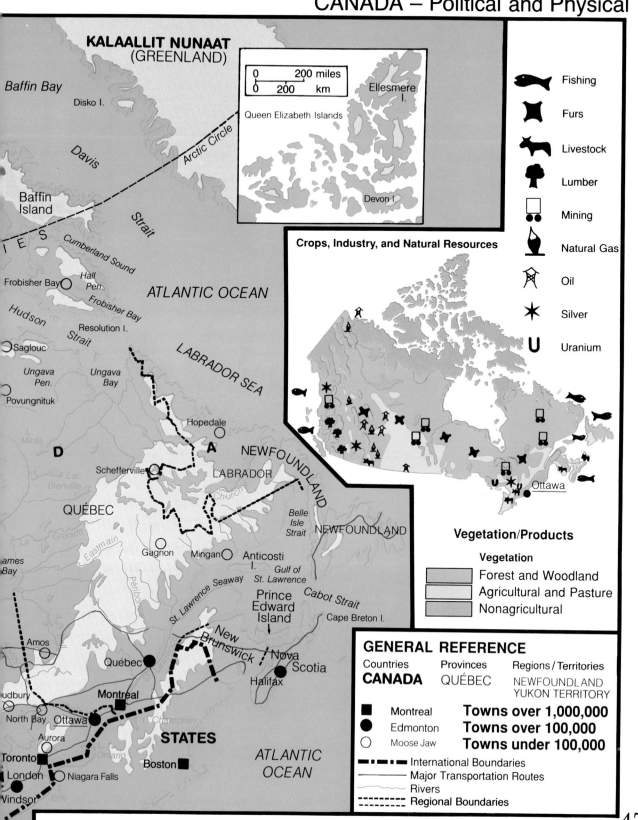

CANADA – Political and Physical

KALAALLIT NUNAAT
(GREENLAND)

Baffin Bay

Disko I.

Davis

Baffin
Island

Strait

I E S

Cumberland Sound

Frobisher Bay

Hall
Pen.

Frobisher Bay

ATLANTIC OCEAN

Hudson

Saglouc

Strait

Resolution I.

*Ungava
Pen.*

*Ungava
Bay*

Povungnituk

LABRADOR SEA

Minto

Hopedale

D

A

NEWFOUNDLAND

Lac
Bienville

Scheffervile

LABRADOR

La Grande

QUÉBEC

Church

ames
Bay

Eastmain

Gagnon

Mingan

Anticosti
I.

*Belle
Isle
Strait*

NEWFOUNDLAND

Péribonka

St. Lawrence Seaway

Gulf of
St. Lawrence

Cabot Strait

Prince
Edward
Island

Cape Breton I.

La

Amos

New
Brunswick

Nova
Scotia

Québec

Halifax

udbury

Montreal

Champlain

North Bay

Ottawa

STATES

ATLANTIC
OCEAN

Aurora

Ontario

Toronto

Boston

London

Niagara Falls

Erie

Vindsor

Scale inset
0	200 miles
0	200 km

Ellesmere
I.

Queen Elizabeth Islands

Devon I.

Arctic Circle

Crops, Industry, and Natural Resources

Ottawa

Legend (Products)
- 🐟 Fishing
- Furs
- Livestock
- Lumber
- Mining
- Natural Gas
- Oil
- Silver
- **U** Uranium

Vegetation/Products

Vegetation
- Forest and Woodland
- Agricultural and Pasture
- Nonagricultural

GENERAL REFERENCE

Countries	Provinces	Regions / Territories
CANADA	QUÉBEC	NEWFOUNDLAND
		YUKON TERRITORY

- ■ Montreal — **Towns over 1,000,000**
- ● Edmonton — **Towns over 100,000**
- ○ Moose Jaw — **Towns under 100,000**

International Boundaries
Major Transportation Routes
Rivers
Regional Boundaries

47

Index